THE LIBERTY OF OBEDIENCE

What the reviewers are saying about

The Liberty of Obedience

"A good thought-provoking book that will help an individual grow to maturity. Well-written and easy to read."

Baptist Sunday School Board

"This is a most descriptive title. By moving through tragedy toward absolute obedience, and from the Atomic Age to the Acuas in the Stone Age, Mrs. Elliot was forced to strip her understanding of her faith and of humanity back to basic Christianity and basic humanity. In the process she moved into the joyous liberty of living by pure love in a world of many enslaving laws and irrelevant traditions. This is a book for meditative reading."

Southwestern Journal of Theology

"This is a small book with a spiritual wallop unequalled by any book I have read recently. It is a book that any Christian, young or old, spiritual babe or leader, will cherish.

THE LIBERTY
of
OBEDIENCE

SOME THOUGHTS ON CHRISTIAN CONDUCT AND SERVICE

ELISABETH ELLIOT

A KEY-WORD BOOK
WORD BOOKS, PUBLISHER
WACO, TEXAS

First Printing—August 1968
Second Printing—December 1968
Third Printing—February 1971

First Key-Word Edition—September 1976

ISBN: 0–87680–831–3
Library of Congress Card Catalog Number: 68–31110
Printed in the United States of America

To my mother,
to whose love and faithfulness
I owe my earliest understanding
of obedience

ACKNOWLEDGMENTS

GRATEFUL ACKNOWLEDGMENT IS MADE TO THE FOLLOWING FOR PERMISSION TO USE COPYRIGHT MATERIAL:

The Division of Christian Education of the National Council of Churches of Christ in the U.S.A.

Quotations from the Revised Standard Version of the Bible (RSV), copyrighted 1946 (renewed 1973), 1956 and 1971 by the Division of Christian Education of the National Council of the Churches of Christ in the U.S.A.

Cambridge University Press

Quotations from *The New English Bible, New Testament,* © The Delegates of the Oxford University Press and The Syndics of The Cambridge University Press, 1961, 1970.

The Macmillan Company

Quotations from *The New Testament in Modern English* translated by J. B. Phillips. Copyright 1947, 1952, 1955, 1957, 1958.

The Sunday School Times and Gospel Herald

For materials previously published in article form.

CONTENTS

FOREWORD

Many people, in their late twenties and early thirties, discover that life is getting more and more complicated. For me it was getting simpler and simpler. I was living with Indians in the forest of Ecuador, and was trying very hard to get down to the root of things because it seemed to me that that was where Indians lived. This process had of course its own complications for me— "simple" cooking over a "simple" wood fire can sometimes be more difficult than fancy cooking on an electric stove—but in matters of importance the direction of my thinking was toward the bare or simple truth. I was for some years almost wholly out of touch with all that had been familiar, and I had therefore a chance to look at it from a long way off, to question and compare.

The tribe that gave me the best chance to do this had been called "savage." They were the Aucas, who by reputation were also "primitive," "godless," "Stone Age" people. They themselves gave me excellent reason to question the accuracy of these terms. They were wonderful people—generous and kind from the very first night of our arrival; capable and intelligent when you saw them in their jungle environment (where white men looked anything but capable and intelligent); amenable (almost touchingly so) to any suggestion from us; eagerly interested in all that we did or said; a people who shared lavishly all they had and were, a people who laughed uproari-

ously most of the time when they were together, and who worked hard when they
were apart (for they did their hunting and
planting usually alone). I found them easy
to love.

It was these very qualities that nettled me.
They simply did not fit my idea of savagery.
What, then, did civilization mean? Was it
merely an efficient method of complicating
things?

For a whole year I watched and learned
and kept my mouth shut. I had to keep my
mouth shut most of the time because I did
not know the Auca language. For once, I
listened and had nothing to say. It was a
valuable exercise, and although the language itself was highly complex, the definition of my task was simple: learn it. I had
just that one thing to do, day after day. No
social engagements, other than the standing
invitation to join the Indians after sundown
when they were all present, talking about

the day's events in exquisite (and, of course, to me usually incomprehensible) detail. I had no "outside" activities. Nothing to complicate my life.

Some of what I learned in that mostly silent year I wrote in a book called *The Savage my Kinsman*.

I spent a second year there, when I had a fairly workable knowledge of the language. I learned more about the Indians, about how they felt and thought, and why they did things the way they did. As a result, more questions were raised in my mind, especially about my own thoughts and feelings and ways of doing things. Often the Auca way seemed better, or at least more defensible if one were to ask, "Why do they do it *this* way?" It was always a sensible and simple way.

Changes were of course inevitable with the presence of foreigners and the coming of airplanes on the strip the Aucas had built.

Complications crept in. I watched this with misgiving, wondering if this were the way it ought to be. Could we not keep things simple? Would not God Himself speak the Word of Truth to the Indians? And would we have the grace to let that Word operate as He wanted it to, or would we hold out our own notions of the effect it should have?

Of changes among these people which could be directly attributed to the power of the Word of Christ I could not honestly say that I knew very much. It seemed to me that this must be a hidden matter of the heart which God alone could rightly assess. I wondered, of course, what sort of visible change I might look for if the Word were being spoken (as, in the last analysis, it can only be spoken) by the Spirit of God. Jesus had said that men can be known by their fruits. I knew the fruits commonly expected by those who had never tried what I was doing. But I could not be satisfied that the changes I was seeing were true fruits. Oddly enough, they were too "simple." Then I began to ask if *I* were making things complicated.

My confusion drove me to the admission that I had not as many answers as I had thought. God kept back some of the ones I wanted, and had other things to say to me. I listened. I studied the Bible, prayed, and thought. Often the Aucas were away all day —hunting and planting—and the clearing was very quiet with only the sound of the little river, the voices of children, or the screech of a parrot.

Why was I here? To "serve the Lord," of course. But what a reply! What an awesome task I had assumed. How was I to do it? What did it mean?

I wanted to give God's Word to the Indians. What, exactly, did this mean? How would that Word be revealed? I wanted desperately to get to the bottom of these issues. I did not want to be misled by prejudices born of my American culture or my church tradition.

So here are "heathen" people, I told myself. And here is the Word of Truth. There must be evidenced among them a recognition of the difference, for example, between good and evil. Would it be the same for them as it was for me? What did God say about it? What would "Christian" conduct mean to the Aucas? I came to see that my own understanding of these subjects was not nearly as clear as I had supposed. I kept balancing the Auca way of life against the American, or against what I had always taken to be the Christian. "By their fruits," Jesus had said. "By their *fruits* ye shall know them." How did they compare?

I have already said that I found the Aucas easy to love, generous, intelligent, happy.

But what of their morals? Here, too, a comparison did not convince me of the superiority of any other group.

I had come from a society where polygamy was illegal to one where it was permissible. Here it seemed to be merely a question of taste. A man might have as many wives as he cared to support at one time, but he did not go and help himself to another man's wife without authorization. In my society a man might neglect even the one wife he had, he might play with other men's wives, and still keep his job and most of his friends. I observed faithfulness and a strong sense of responsibility on the part of Auca husbands. Was this comparison an argument in favor of polygamy? Were there Scriptural arguments against it?

One expects to find savages cruel. I found cruelty among the Aucas, but they found it in me, too. In America a man who switched a naked child with nettles would be called a sadist. Aucas considered this a legitimate and effective form of punishment, and were outraged to see me spank my three-year-old child. I was, to them, a savage. I realized after a while that neither action was necessarily motivated by cruelty, nor did it do any permanent damage. In our own country certain forms of cruelty are tolerated, others are not. But were the Aucas not killers? They were, but let us not forget that in our society it is permissible to murder a man not only in one's heart, but also by verbally cutting him to pieces before his friends. Aucas had not been acquainted with this method.

In my country we hold certain standards of dress to be acceptable (for a few months or a year at a time), but a costume that would have landed its wearer in jail one year might be common on the streets of a city the next. The Aucas were unhampered by clothing (or by washing, sewing, mending, or ironing) and the caprices of fashion (with the vanity, jealousy, covetousness and discontent which fashion fosters), but stuck firmly to a code of modesty which did not change with the seasons. In their nakedness they accepted themselves and one another for what they were, always abiding by the rules: men and women did not bathe together, women taught their daughters how to sit and stand with modesty, men taught their sons how to wear the string which was their only adornment. Physiological functions were discussed in public but performed in strictest privacy.

I saw the Indians live in a harmony which far surpassed anything I had seen among those who call themselves Christians. I found that even their killing had at least as valid reasons as the wars in which my people engaged. "By their fruits . . ."

Could I really offer them a better way? Jesus said, "I am the Way." He, therefore, was the one responsible to show what it was for them. I was merely His representative, and I had better be very sure I knew what He did actually say about the questions of conduct and service, for it was to Him above all others that I must give account.

In an attempt to find out, and to sort out my own convictions and give clear expression to them, I studied the New Testament and especially the Epistles of Paul. What I found seemed to me to be important not only for me in that unusual place, but for Christians everywhere, so I wrote for *The Sunday School Times* the series of brief articles which is reprinted here. In the six years since I left that particular thatched house, I have been questioned and sometimes challenged on these matters. Each time my answer has been along the lines written during those days in Tewaenon. But it was my husband who first taught me to question and examine, and then to act on what one believes. He first showed me what liberty in

Christ means. Perhaps now, many years after his death, I am beginning to grasp things he understood. He glimpsed, I think, something of the largeness of God's heart and wanted to show it to others.

I can add nothing to the statement of the issues set forth here. This is what I believe. Why I believe it, why the issues became inescapable for me at the time, I have tried to explain in the introduction to each chapter. I hope that the introductions may help the reader to gain for himself the same perspective which clarified for me the alternatives.

FRANCONIA, NEW HAMPSHIRE

I

WHAT IS MEANT BY

THE APPEARANCE OF EVIL?

If it is a difficult thing to live above reproach in one's society where values are judged at least similarly, how much more difficult it is in another culture. Each society has its own way of expressing itself, and what looks like sin in one context may look like virtue in another. The Aucas were convinced, for reasons they themselves could not give, that outsiders were cannibals.

Quite naturally, then, they were prepared to interpret the behavior of any outsider they might meet as characteristic of a cannibal. When five missionary men met the Aucas on a sand strip of the Curaray River, they tried in every way they knew to show the Indians that they were friendly. One of the missionaries put his arm around an Auca man, a gesture which to us cannot be understood in any way other than friendliness. Years later I learned from the Aucas themselves that they had taken this to be proof of the foreigner's being a cannibal. It was a gesture that had no meaning for an Auca, and therefore must be a gesture common to cannibals. What looks like love to us looked like hostility to the Aucas. Jesus' love for common men led Him to eat and drink with them, and for this He was called a glutton and a winebibber, a friend of publicans and sinners.

"To the pure, all things are pure."

Clearly, it is not possible to behave in a way which would be understood by all, let alone accepted by all. God alone, who is above all and in us all, judges rightly, and therefore it is before Him that we stand or fall.

A sincere attempt to discover ways in which I might guide the Aucas in making moral choices led me to the realization that I had sometimes called things sinful which the Bible did not call sinful; and if I had imposed these on the Indians, I would have been guilty of the Pharisees' sin of laying burdens too heavy to be borne. It may take a new kind of courage for us to believe that God must interpret His Word to His people. We may find ourselves on the wrong side of some man-made fences, but this is a part of the risk of following Him without reservation, of doing the truth, and of unconditionally committing our case to God.

I

WHAT IS MEANT BY

THE APPEARANCE OF EVIL?

"Don't do anything that might look like sin to somebody else." This is a modern translation of what is often understood by Paul's injunction to the Thessalonians, "Abstain from all appearance of evil" (1 Thess. 5:22). Is this what Paul meant? Let us carefully note some examples of behavior given in Scripture, and then decide whether this interpretation is valid.

When the Syrian army commander Naa-

man was cured of his leprosy, he acknowl-
edged Israel's God as the only true one. He
immediately thought of his responsibility in
the service of a pagan king. A part of this
service was to accompany the king to the
worship of his god. Naaman declared that
from henceforth his own loyalty would be to
the true God, but he must perform his duty
to his earthly master. Elisha, the man of
God, assured him that he might go in peace.
What of the "testimony"? What of the criticism that might come because he "contrib-
uted" to the king's idolatry? Elisha simply
said, "Go in peace."

There was one occasion when Peter,
though newly aware of the liberty which
God had given him in revealing that the gospel was for Gentile as well as Jew, felt that
he must abstain from eating with Gentiles
for fear of offending the Jews. To eat with
uncircumcised men would present the appearance of evil to the law-abiding Jews.

This decision was serious enough to warrant Paul's public rebuke.

The Lord Jesus frequently offended the sensibilities of religious leaders. They could not conscientiously approve the company He kept; He condoned law-breaking (was this not indisputably "sin"?) in allowing His disciples to gather corn on the Sabbath, or to pull an ox out of a ditch; He gained for Himself the reputation of the "Prince of Evil" (Matt. 10:25, Phillips).

On other occasions, although doing nothing which could be called sin, He refused to do things which were called good—for example, He deliberately left doubt in the minds of questioners; He told certain ones who had been healed to be quiet about it; He refused to give signs to prove His power or identity; He did not condemn the adulterous woman. Small wonder that righteous eyebrows were raised and orthodox consciences outraged.

Paul says of those who attempted to "tie us with rules and regulations" (concerning circumcision of Gentiles), "We did not give those men an inch, for the truth of the Gospel for you and for all Gentiles was at stake." Although just prior to this statement he tells how he had conferred with the church leaders to be sure that what he did was acceptable to *them,* he shows here that the opinions of the religious legalists mattered not at all to him. The issue at stake was much higher.

There were times when the Lord purposely acted so as not to offend. The tax collectors presumed that He would not pay the Temple tax. Jesus was legally exempt, but His reply to Peter's question was, "We don't want to give offense to these people," and He told him how to obtain the money to pay the tax.

Later the Pharisees appealed to Jesus on the basis of a fact they knew to be true—

that He did not care for human approval—
and asked Him if one should pay his tax to
Caesar. It was a shrewd question. They received a shrewd answer. Yes. The tax was
rightfully Caesar's. It should be paid. This
matter of civic duty did not run contrary to
man's duty to God.

If on one occasion we avoid what others
may say is sin, and on another consider a
similar act the right thing to do, how are we
to understand the King James rendering of
Paul's command? If to abstain from the appearance of evil does not mean to shun
everything that someone else may call sin,
what does it mean?

Several translations may help us to see
what Paul was emphasizing (1 Thess. 5:21,
22). The context concerns inspiration and
prophetic utterances. We are not to despise
them, but to test them. From the results of
our test, we are to choose the good and refuse the bad, whatever form it may take.

The Revised Standard Version says, "Test everything; hold fast what is good, abstain from every form of evil." The New English Bible, "Bring them all to the test and then keep what is good in them and avoid the bad of whatever kind." Phillips translates as follows: "By all means use your judgment, and hold on to whatever is really good. Steer clear of evil in any form."

There is no question but that our Lord "steered clear of evil in any form." This did not prevent some from accusing Him of evil. His concern was to do the thing that pleased His Father. If He could at the same time avoid offense, He did. If in being obedient, He at times horrified men of high reputation —indeed, of religious reputation—and appeared to be acting contrary to the law of God, He counted it of no consequence.

Paul wrote to the Romans, "Don't become set in your own opinions . . . Don't say, 'It doesn't matter what people think,' but see that your public behavior is above criticism" (Rom. 12:17, Phillips). In perhaps the most quoted passage of all, Romans 14:16, where Paul stresses our responsibility to the weak brother's conscience, he says "You mustn't let something that is all right for you look like an evil practice to somebody else" (Phillips). Yet he had told Peter to eat with the Gentiles whether the Jews liked it or not.

What is the answer? One incident dealt with the ceremonial uncleanness of what is eaten, the other with the ceremonial uncleanness of the company in which it is eaten. In each case it seems that the universality of the Gospel was at stake. God had cleansed all food, and given Christians liberty to eat it without asking questions for conscience's sake; and He had cleansed all races as well, and given them liberty to associate freely in His name. Yet the advice given by Paul seems directly contradictory in the two cases.

To the Corinthians he said, "It matters

very little to me what you, or any man thinks of me. . . . My only true judge is the Lord" (1 Cor. 4:3, 4, Phillips). But in speaking of the distribution of the church funds, he said, "Naturally we want to avoid the slightest breath of criticism . . . and to be absolutely aboveboard not only in the sight of God but in the eyes of man" (2 Cor. 8:20, 21, Phillips). And finally, in his plea to the Romans to recognize how varied may be the behavior of men who are equally desirous of pleasing God, he writes, "Why, then, criticize your brother's actions, why try to make him look small? We shall all be judged one day, not by one another's standards or even our own, but by the judgment of God . . . It is to God alone that we have to answer for our actions" (Rom. 14:10, 12, Phillips).

We shall answer for our actions. Were they good or evil? We cannot answer for others' opinions of our actions. An act should be done not for the sake of the reputation it will gain or destroy for a man, but because it is right. If it appears wrong to some, this is only fresh proof of the impossibility of man's looking on the heart. This is God's prerogative. He alone knows, in any given case, whether the individual has honestly considered what others may think, and whether that consideration has affected the action.

There is no rule of thumb as to whether it ought to affect the action. *Decisions must be made in the integrity of the heart before God—with an unselfish attention to our brother's good and the glory of God.* None of us is capable of plumbing even his own motives, far less those of his brother, so let us be slow to criticize another. Let us not be Pharisees in our certainty of what God could or could not permit.

II

ALL THINGS ARE YOURS

Could an Auca be worldly? This was a question that came to me with annoying frequency as I watched them in their daily work, conversation, and relationships. The difficulty of answering the question pointed to the difficulty of defining what the Bible means by worldliness. Perhaps it is not really difficult, perhaps it was only because I was so thoroughly conditioned to think of worldliness in special terms that I found it difficult. I had been taught—in a Christian home, in Christian schools and college— that certain activities, certain modes of eating and drinking and dressing, certain places, were "worldly." As I sat in my hammock in Tewaenon, I went over these rules, trying to decide how, if at all, they might apply to the Auca people, or, if they did not apply, whether I was justified in applying them to anyone, and what rules might be relevant for Aucas and the rest of us.

If the Gospel necessarily brings certain kinds of change in one people—twentieth century Americans, for instance—will it operate in the same way among another people —Stone Age Indians, for instance? Does the Gospel change? Does it always have the same effect? Had we perhaps confused tradition with the truth of God? Had we categorized where the Spirit of God meant us to be free?

Some groups of Christians in civilized America believe it to be important to dress in a certain way. How was one to regard this view of worldliness in a society where no one dressed at all? If the Auca was to put on clothes, was he to put on a certain kind?

Such questions began to appear more and more absurd to me, and in all honesty I had to confront them on the basis of Scripture, asking not "What will people think?" or "What will this do to the work?" but "What does God specifically say?"

This is what I found.

II

ALL THINGS ARE YOURS

"I am in earnest about forsaking 'the world' and following Christ. But I am puzzled about worldly things. What is it I must forsake?" a young man asks.

"Colored clothes, for one thing. Get rid of everything in your wardrobe that is not white. Stop sleeping on a soft pillow. Sell your musical instruments and don't eat any more white bread. You cannot, if you are sincere about obeying Christ, take warm baths or shave your beard. To shave is to lie against Him who created us, to attempt to improve on His work."

Does this answer sound absurd? It is the answer given in the most celebrated Christian schools of the second century! Is it possible that the rules that have been adopted by many twentieth-century Christians will sound as absurd to earnest followers of Christ a few years hence?

Paul, as early as A.D. 62, wrote a letter to a small group of believers who had been plagued by some who set up rules and regulations concerning "worldly" things. The Colossians, in a sincere effort to forsake the world, had submitted to these rules, and in so doing had actually made themselves part of the world-system. Paul wrote to show them how completely they had missed the point. The prohibitions concerned purely temporary things ("Don't touch this," "Don't taste that," and "Don't handle the other," as J. B. Phillips translates Colos-

sians 2:21). Throw them off, says Paul—
they look wise, they promote an exertion of
will power, but they are worthless in check-
ing the indulgence of the flesh. They have
nothing to do with the real issue.

What is the issue? It is just here that the
Colossians, and we, have made such lamen-
table mistakes. The Scripture means two
things by the expression, "the world." First,
and most simply, it means all that is temporal. Second, and by implication, it means
all those who are occupied solely with the
temporal. The first category comprises
things; the second, people.

What are "worldly" things? All inanimate objects are worldly. They will pass
away. Paul uses food and the stomach as
examples. "God has no permanent purpose
for either" (1 Cor. 6:13, Phillips). Marriage is referred to as a "worldly distrac-
tion," that is, it is a temporal institution, and
not to be the ultimate object of our concern.

Paul personally felt that others would be better off if they followed his example in this matter and remained single. But he did not forbid marriage, and certainly our Lord not only allowed it, He hallowed it.

The holy place, under the first covenant, is referred to by one source as a "worldly holy place," a temporal one (Heb. 9:1).

It is remarkable that the Lord Jesus, who was very much of a non-conformist in spirit, thought, and teaching, conformed to the world in matters of food, drink, and dress, and even in social situations. Although little is said about Him in connection with these things, what is recorded indicates that there was nothing distinctive about His practices. He ate what other people ate, drank what they drank—and even in questionable company, and in such a manner that He was accused of being a glutton and a drunkard.

Surely He dressed as other men dressed if He was not easily recognized on many occasions. (He even had to be identified by Judas' kiss.) The one garment about which we are told must have been of the currently acceptable cut, or it is doubtful whether soldiers would have quibbled over it, despite its superior quality (woven without seam).

On one striking occasion Jesus attended a village wedding. The Son of God went to a party. Not only did He go, but He worked a miracle so that the guests could have second servings of wine when the supply failed.

What did John mean by telling us not to love the world, or the things in it? What does Romans 12 mean by conformity to the world? The answer lies in the verbs used, not in the noun "world." We are to be transformed by the renewing—not of our hairdo, or of our menu—but of our *minds*.

Every man is ultimately concerned with something. He has given his heart, his allegiance, to something—set his direction. Thus the Scripture speaks of the "godly" man in the Psalms, the man whose heart is ready to seek God. His counterpart has set his heart to seek things which are going to pass away. No man can be headed in two directions at one time.

Jesus Christ gave us, with Himself, all *things* freely to enjoy. Paul reminded us that all things are ours. We are not asked to deny ourselves as many things as possible in order to set our hearts on the Eternal. Things are not incompatible with Christ. They are all "worldly," in the simplest sense—they are for this world. They are not sinful for this reason. Only human beings may be sinful, or "worldly" in the most precise interpretation of that word.

It is not what goes into the man that defiles him. It is what comes out. It is our use of things that determines their effect on us. It is our response to events, not the events themselves, that shapes us. God is more concerned with the heart. He is not as concerned that we obey a code of conduct governing outward things. He says, "My Son, give me thine heart."

Every moment of our lives we are faced with spiritual hazards, and at the same time with spiritual opportunities. How do I as an individual respond to everything presented to me? Let us take a very common example. I come to the table. Food presents a hazard —I may become gluttonous. The food itself is not wrong, but I may use it unwisely.

Jesus taught self-control and exemplified it in His own walk on earth. The fact that some have destroyed themselves by the wrong use of food is not sufficient reason for the rest of us to fast. Paul told Timothy, "Every creature of God is good, and nothing to be refused, if it be received with thanksgiving: for it is sanctified by the word of God and prayer."

Food, therefore, may be "sanctified" if eaten by a man who loves God and thanks

Him for it. Let us give our hearts, not to food, not to expensive clothes, but to Him who gave us everything—give it to the Creator, not to His creation.

We have said that all *things* are worldly, that the Scripture does not therefore call them sinful. We refer to inanimate objects. We do have some lists, however, in Colossians and James of worldly things that are condemned. Let us be very careful to note that these are not material things—they are characteristics of people, that is, they are specific sins. We are to put to death these worldly (or "earthly") things, since we have been raised from the dead with Christ Himself, and we no longer have any business with immorality, impurity, evil desire, covetousness, anger, malice, slander, foul talk, lying. James lists, under the "contamination of the world," rivalry, bitter jealousy, disharmony. These spring from a desire for "things" that the world can provide, such as acclaim and status. God's wisdom, on the other hand, is characterized by purity, peace, gentleness, approachability, tolerance, kindly actions, impartiality, sincerity.

Let us try to keep matters straight and not make a "trial of God," as some men from Judea did in the matter of outward circumcision (Acts 15) by putting a yoke upon the necks of others. Let us see clearly what the Bible means by worldliness and limit our definition to that. Paul's plea to the Colossians to forget the man-made rules regarding earthly things is followed by a far more impassioned plea for compassion, kindness, lowliness, meekness, patience, forbearance, forgiveness, and love. Let peace rule. Be thankful. Let the Word of Christ dwell in you. Do everything in the name of the Lord Jesus.

III

THE HIGHEST FORM

OF SERVICE

There has often been a tendency to think of service to God as necessarily entailing physical hardship and sacrifice. Although this is not really a Scriptural idea, it has gained wide acceptance. It is easy to recall the saints who climbed the steep ascent of heaven through peril, toil, and pain, but the Bible also makes mention of Dorcas whose service to God was the making of coats.

(*And who can tell what pain she knew that is not recorded? It is God who keeps tears in His bottle.*)

When I lived in the Auca settlement, there were some who, from a long distance and with little idea of the actual situation, commended me for my "wonderful work," probably because they thought of it as difficult, isolated, dangerous, or even sacrificial. There were others who for the very same reason condemned me, for I had taken a three-year-old child into that setting. Some envied me, some pitied me. Some admired, some criticized. I could not help asking myself if perhaps I had been mistaken. Was I really obeying God, or had I merely obeyed some misguided impulse, some lust for distinction, some masochistic urge to bury myself in the forsaken place? There was no way of being sure what was in the murky reaches of my subconscious, but I was sure I had committed myself to God for His service, and I knew no other motivation. The opinions of others—whether they commended or condemned—could not alter my duty, but their very diversity caused me to ponder carefully what that duty was.

And then, by contrast, I watched the Indians, doing things they understood, untroubled by questions of "service" to God or fellow-men (although they had served me in countless ways—and I thought of the King saying to them, "Inasmuch as ye have done it unto one of the least of these . . . ye have done it unto me," and of how surprised they would be when they knew), free of the pressures of competition and comparison. There was for me here a lesson in simplicity and acceptance of one's place in life, which I, because I was a Christian, could take from the hand of God.

My duty was one thing, theirs another. My responsibility lay here, but the responsibility of some of my correspondents who *gazed starry-eyed at my role lay perhaps in an office or a kitchen or the cockpit of an airplane. Who was to say which deserved to sit on God's right hand?*

III

THE HIGHEST FORM

OF SERVICE

"I wish I were giving my life to the Lord. I give myself many excuses—my unsaved wife, my unsaved children, my job. I have no Christian companions. I work from 8 to 4:30 every day, with 150 people, and not one Christian among them. Nothing ever satisfies this longing that I be really used by the Lord. You are the one who is in the thick of the really important things in life. . . ." This is from a letter I received recently. It is not the first of its kind that has disturbed me deeply—not because the man does not have a chance to serve God, but because he does not see his chance. He has missed the true meaning of "being used by the Lord." What actually *are* the "really important things?"

One clear statement of what God considers important is given in Paul's letter to the Ephesians: "He purposes in his sovereign will that all human history shall be consummated in Christ, that everything that exists in Heaven or earth shall find its perfection and fulfillment in him" (Eph. 1:9, 10, Phillips). Perfection, fulfillment—maturity. The completion of the Body of Christ in final union and perfect love is the Father's plan.

The immensity of such a plan has perhaps so overwhelmed some of us that we are tempted to feel that there is no way for "poor little me" to contribute to it. And

—most unfortunately—the over-balanced publicity some segments of Christendom have given to foreign missions, or home missions, or soul-winning, have led some to feel that the people who are engaged in that type of work are, if not the only "real" servants of God, surely by far the most "important."

If the Bible says anything about the relative importance of certain types of service, it is that we human beings are generally mistaken as to which they are. Jesus told us that we should expect some surprises when the truth is finally made known. The last are going to be first. He gave us an illustration of how unpredictable the rewards are likely to be in the parable of the foreman who paid all the laborers the same wage, regardless of whether they had worked one hour or one whole day.

All Christians are members of a Body—parts with specific functions to fulfill. Who can assess the relative importance of physical organs? In our English-speaking culture we are accustomed to thinking of the heart as the most vital organ. It is figuratively the seat of the affections, but to the Quichua Indian of Ecuador it is the liver that is filled with love. Which is the more indispensable? The God who designed the human body with its interdependent functions also designed the Body of Christ, and He has given to each member not only a special place and service but a gift as well.

If we adequately understand these facts, we must honestly acknowledge that we have no excuse for "not having used," or for not doing, the "really important things," either because of circumstances (e.g., an unsaved wife, a lonely job, health, finances, age, geographical location, or anything else) or because of not being gifted.

"In each of us the Spirit is manifested in one particular way, for some useful purpose" (1 Cor. 12:7, N.E.B.). This one short verse shows us that:

Each has a gift.
     It comes from God.
   It is distinct from others'.
   It has a definite object.

Those who emphasize their inabilities do an injustice to the grace of God, which has dispensed gifts to all. And they are guilty, as well, of a lack of gratitude and a sense of responsibility. There are the opposite, too —those to whom Paul wrote, "Don't cherish exaggerated ideas of yourself or your importance, but try to have a sane estimate of your capabilities by the light of the faith that God has given to you all" (Rom. 12:3, Phillips). What sorrow, frustration, and sickening failure result from the attempt to do a job for which one was never fitted. If we allow ourselves to worship some hero and try to imitate him, we may be exaggerating our own importance. If we refuse to budge, on the other hand, because we belittle the gift God has given us, we are equally guilty. We are not making a sane estimate.

I received another letter, very different from the first one I quoted. This was a prayer letter from a missionary candidate. She was not going to the mission field after all.

"After a second interview . . . . I have faced and admitted that I lack the most vital qualification for the work among the Muslims, namely, a vital, deep-seated, quiet assurance and confidence in Christ. My faith is rather superficial and untested; therefore, I feel it best to withdraw my application.

"The Lord has exposed many hidden motives. My desire to go to the Muslim was motivated by personal ambition coupled with a vague sense of guilt and condemnation if I did not become a foreign missionary. How thankful I am that God stopped me."

If each of us has a gift, we know that its source had to be God. James told us this.

"Every good endowment that we possess and every complete gift that we have received must come from above, from the Father of all lights" (Jas. 1:17, Phillips). To receive a gift and then ignore its source is not only the most chilling ingratitude, it is sheer arrogance. We give ourselves—or perhaps our heritage, or our education (which amounts to the same thing)—the credit. "If anything has been given to you, why boast of it as if it were something you had achieved yourself?" (1 Cor. 4:7, Phillips). In the definitive chapter on spiritual gifts, 1 Corinthians 12, there is a notable repetition of the phrases, "of the Spirit," "by the Spirit," and "through the Spirit." Peter, too, reminds us that "in whatever way a man serves the Church he should do it recognizing the fact that God gives him his ability, so that God *may be glorified in everything* through Jesus Christ" (1 Pet. 4:11, Phillips, italics mine). The gift's source and end is God. To ignore the one is to frustrate the other.

God's gifts are richly varied. How insufferably dull it would be if they were not! "After all, if the body were all one eye, for example, where would be the sense of hearing? Or if it were all one ear, where would be the sense of smell?" (1 Cor. 12:17, Phillips). We have emphasized above that it is "through the grace *of God* that we have different gifts." Let us emphasize now that it is through the grace of God that we have *different* gifts. Yet how wistfully we look at another's gift and wish we could do that. How pitiably we say to ourselves, "If only I had his brains" (or faith, or energy, or voice, or courage, or looks, or executive talents). We were never meant to have it. God saw what He wanted to do, and He equipped each of us accordingly, and woe to us if we spend our time fruitlessly wishing we were eyes when we were made hands.

The prayer letter quoted above goes on:

"As was . . . . so kindly pointed out to me, 'In a great house there are not only vessels of gold and silver, but also [utensils] of wood and earthenware, and some for honorable and noble [use] and some for menial and ignoble [use]' (2 Tim. 2:20, Amp. N.T.).

"Self-seekingly, I desired to be an honorable and noble vessel—not a menial and ignoble vessel. Egotistically, I coveted being elegant cut glass; whereas, God made me common earthenware. Secretly, I dreamed of being another Mary Slessor, Praying Hyde, David Brainerd, and Amy Carmichael all rolled into one. . . ."

We envy one man's place in the Body, and we disdain another's. We think one man is doing the *great* thing, and we fail to see how another can possibly be of any use in what we call "the Lord's service." It is understandable that the eye might feel like saying to the hand, "I don't need you," but the eye's failure to perceive the usefulness of the hand proves nothing. Paul gave us the most obvious illustration he could think of. Yet we persist in setting up our own hierarchy of values, lionizing one for the mere performance of his duty, and degrading another because his is not "really important." Or, to put it more graphically, we praise the eye because it can see, and we condemn the hand because it cannot see. We have nothing to do with the choice of the gift. We have everything to do with the use of the gift. Remember the parable of the servants and what they did with the talents.

Some of the gifts listed in the New Testament are preaching, serving others, teaching, stimulating faith, giving, exercising authority, giving sympathy, speaking with wisdom, putting knowledge into words, faith, healing, power to do great deeds, discriminating between spirits, speaking in tongues, interpreting tongues, and helping. (Note the last, "helping," is a gift.) This is only an indication of the magnificent diversity of talents which the Creator of personalities has dispensed. We are to appraise our own talent intelligently, and exercise it, Paul says, "according to the proportion of our faith," (Rom. 12:6, A.S.V.), heartily, energetically, and cheerfully. Elsewhere he adds "intelligently" (1 Cor. 14:15, N.E.B.), and "decently and in order."

The proper use of our gifts in service to one another is the Scriptural meaning of "serving the Lord," of "being used," of giving one's life to God. For this—and this alone—truly leads to the maturity of the Body. "And these were his gifts: . . . to equip God's people for work in his service, to the building up of the body of Christ. So shall we all at last attain to the unity inherent in our faith and our knowledge of the Son of God—to mature manhood, measured by nothing less than the full stature of Christ . . . Bonded and knit together by every constituent joint, the whole frame grows through the due activity of each part, and builds itself up in love" (Eph. 4:11–16, N.E.B.). Love—the best gift, the highest to be attained, the one gift above all other gifts that leads the individual and ultimately the Church to maturity.

IV

Maturity: The Power

to Discern

A missionary friend of mine once said, "Things were simple before I went to Africa. I knew what the African's problem was, and I knew the answer. When I got there and began to know him as a person, things were no longer simple." When, on the first night of our arrival in the "savage" Aucas' village, they gave us houses to live in, food and water and wood and fire, things were not so simple for me. My categories began to crumble. I had thought I knew what a savage was like. I had thought I knew exactly how the gospel would change him. As weeks passed, I began to realize that not only had I been mistaken about these things, but very likely I was just as mistaken about some other categories which had seemed clear before. How readily I had seen Christian virtues in those I called Christians in my own country, and the "works of the flesh" in those who did not bear the Christian label. What was I now to do with the apparent manifestation of virtue—peace, longsuffering, kindness—in those who had never heard of Christ? Things were not what I had thought. What was I to do then? Should I reject facts? Or should I begin to trust God in a new acceptance of my own ignorance and His saving responsibility?

When I have tried to tell people truth-

fully what I found among the Aucas, I have sometimes been asked (with a hint of hostility), "Well, what are you trying to say?" I am trying to say what is, and it is for us to bring to bear upon these facts, as upon all the facts of our existence, the light of our faith. If there are inexplicables, if there are ambiguities, they are but new stations in our pilgrimage, and we have a Leader, the Pioneer and Perfecter of our faith, who wants us to follow Him to maturity.

IV

Maturity: The Power

to Discern

"Sin is sin, no matter when, where, or by whom committed." "If it's doubtful, it's dirty." So says the man who sees all things in black or white. There is no question in his mind about right and wrong. He knows. He knows not only what he must do, but what his brother must do—or, if he does not go quite so far, he knows at least what his brother must not do. He says, "I don't see how so-and-so could possibly do *that* for the glory of God."

79

Does the Scripture teach that sin is sin, in the sense that what is sin for one man is always sin for all? It does *not*. In fact it shows that what may be sin in one man may glorify God in another.

How then are we to know? "It is easy to think that we 'know' over problems like this [i.e., eating meat sacrificed to idols], but we should remember that while knowledge may make a man look big, it is only love that can make him grow to his full stature. For whatever a man may know, he still has a lot to learn; but if he loves God, he is opening his whole life to the Spirit of God" (1 Cor. 8:1, Phillips translation).

This is fundamental. We must admit that we do *not* know all the answers about good and evil. We cannot always tell what is sin. But if we love God, we have begun to learn. We are on the way to maturity.

Who are the mature? Hebrews 5:14 says they are "those who by reason of use (practice) have their senses exercised to discern both good and evil." It does not take practice to read a rule book. It may take time to memorize it, and a longer time to follow it, but to see which rule says "do" and which says "do not" is simple. It does not call for discernment.

A child may learn very quickly that if he spills his milk he will be scolded. A monkey may learn that if he pulls a certain rope he will get a banana. But these are not signs of a mature mind. It is important, of course, that the child learn not to spill his milk. But as he grows older, the efforts of his parents are concentrated not on Johnny's remembering to wipe his feet or pick up his clothes (i.e., the family "rule book"—necessary, but not adequate), but on teaching him to discern, to think; not on forcing him to agree with their choices, but on teaching him to make his own.

God the Father intends to make of His

children spiritual adults. He has called us sons. It is a far different thing to train a son. The servant is employed for a specific task. He is told exactly how and when to perform it. He has very little liberty to exercise his own preferences. The son is not trained for a job, but for a life.

If we as Christians regard the Bible as a list of unequivocal rules, we obscure or even annul this training. The Ten Commandments, when given, appeared to be unequivocal. They were written on stone. But God soon showed His people that they must not assume they had heard the last word. There was need for interpretation, for discernment, for understanding, even of these apparent absolutes. They could not henceforth dispense with the voice of His Spirit and the discipline of His instruction. "Thou shalt not kill"—except under certain conditions: except, for example, when God required His chosen people to wipe out an enemy, including women and children.

"Thou shalt not commit adultery"—unless God commands it. Could He command a thing He also forbade? He asked Hosea (a mature man who knew God and could be trusted) to marry a harlot. This is an extreme case, but one alone is sufficient to illustrate the answer to the disturbing question. He could, indeed, command a hitherto forbidden thing. How shall we be prepared for the shock of such cases? How, if God should require of us an unthinkable thing, shall we recognize this requirement? Again and again in Scripture individual men heard the voice of the Lord calling them to do His bidding, and again and again they obeyed in defiance of human logic and law. The Pharisees, religious and learned men, were not prepared for the blast of truth from the Living Word. They had the written word to support every argument, and they accused Jesus of Sabbath-breaking. They ended up at last by killing Him.

In the early church there were arguments

about morality. Paul pointed out in one instance that a man might eat a plate of food for the glory of God, and another man might glorify God by abstaining from the same food.

It appears that God has deliberately left us in a quandary about many things. Why did He not summarize all the rules in one book, and all the basic doctrines in another? He could have eliminated the loopholes, prevented all the schisms over morality and false teaching that have plagued His Church for two thousand years. Think of the squabbling and perplexity we would have been spared. And think of the crop of dwarfs He would have reared!

He did not spare us. He wants us to reach maturity. He has so arranged things that if we are to go on beyond the "milk diet" we shall be forced to think. We must train our faculties by practice to distinguish between good and evil. We are fond of quoting Romans 8:28. But this verse is nearly meaningless without its following verse, in which lies another definition of maturity, "to be shaped to the likeness of his son" (N.E.B.). Unless we see this as the true "good" referred to in verse 28, we shall wonder how Paul can possibly have been so naïve. We shall be forced to regard him—perhaps with affection and certainly with pity—as a misguided Pollyanna, trying to prove to himself that there is always something to be glad about, and shutting his eyes to the sad and the bad. But, given the definition of verse 29, we see that all our spiritual education is directed toward God's idea of good, this "conformity to Christ."

Note that He is not interested in conformity to a static code but to a person, the "likeness of His Son," the living expression of Himself, the very Life of all the ages. This is a far cry from a stereotype. Had God given us a minute prescription for our behavior, no high development of individual character would have been necessary to meet it. He need not have mentioned discernment. But the Law, said the writer to the Hebrews, was incapable of bringing anyone to maturity. The "letter"—for example, a rule book, a code, a policy—is deadening. It cannot stimulate growth.

Do we find here a clue to the immaturity so evident among Christians? Paul found immaturity among the Corinthians, manifested in their jealousy and party spirit. They had subscribed to certain groups— one of Paul, one of Apollos, one of Christ. Each felt that his group had the truth, that they were right. It naturally followed that those who did not "belong" must be wrong.

Too many Christians in this century base their decisions on organizational policy, or on a set of regulations, perhaps unwritten, but tacitly accepted by their particular group. Some are too ready to equate the will of the board with the will of God. They sigh in relief at being thus absolved from the personal responsibility which they are not mature enough to assume. It is too difficult to make decisions that involve doctrine and morality. How much less demanding to sign someone else's statement. This requires no private inquiry with God, and involves small risk of criticism or betrayal, since "the group" approves. Many a painful personal encounter can be avoided with, "It is our policy . . ."

But no policy can encompass in advance the difficult paths through which God may lead a soul to maturity. The man who determines to go on to perfection must go on alone. The child must learn independence. James wrote that when endurance is fully developed "you will find you have become men of mature character with the right sort of independence" (Jas. 1:4, Phillips translation).

No two persons are subject to the same tests. Each must endure the tests alone and each must respond individually. Paul said, "It is important that we go forward in the light of such truth as we have *ourselves* attained to" (Phil. 3:16, Phillips, italics mine). Jesus spoke of having much truth that His disciples could not then bear. He knew where they were spiritually. He knows our progress now, and He knows how to speak to the heart. We err in trying to conform to another's thinking. "Don't let the world around you squeeze you into its own mold," said Paul, "but let God remold your minds from within, so that you may prove in practice that the plan of God for you is good, meets all his demands and moves toward the goal of true maturity" (Rom. 12:2, 3, Phillips).

This was Paul's personal goal, though he stated it even more comprehensively, "to know him." For to know Christ is to be made like Him. It is in beholding the image that we are changed into it, transformed by what we love.

Maturity was Paul's goal for others as well. "We warn everyone we meet, and we teach everyone we can, all that we know about him, so that, if possible, we may bring every man up to his full maturity in Christ Jesus. This is what I am working at all the time, with all the strength that God gives me" (Col. 1:28, Phillips). His fellow worker, Epaphras, shared his vision: "He prays constantly and earnestly for you, that you may become mature Christians, and may fulfill God's will for you" (Col. 4:12, Phillips).

Let us who claim to take the Bible as our norm not oversimplify. Our search for truth has by no means ended—although our facile mouthing of formulas could turn away some who are earnestly seeking. We have much to seek and much to learn. We are meant to "hold firmly to the truth in love, *and* to grow up in every way into Christ" (Eph. 4:14, 15, Phillips, italics mine).

God is absolute. His Word is authority. Still, it is at the same time anything but cut and dried.

> For the Love of God is broader,
>   Than the measure of man's mind;
> And the heart of the Eternal
>   Is most wonderfully kind.
>
> But we make His love too narrow,
>   By false limits of our own
> And we magnify its strictness,
>   With a zeal He will not own.
>   Frederick W. Faber

As sons of God developing into maturity, we shall expect to be corrected in the process, and though this will be unpleasant, "when it is all over we can see that it has quietly produced the fruit of real goodness in the characters of those who have accepted it in the right spirit" (Heb. 12:11, Phillips). And with reference to the difficulties that are part of our daily education for maturity, Paul says, "Taken in the right spirit these very things will give us patient endurance; this in turn will develop a mature character, and a character of this sort produces a steady hope, a hope that will never disappoint us" (Rom. 5:5, Phillips). That marvelous hope—that we *shall* yet reach that ultimate end of all creation, fulfillment— maturity in Christ, for "everything that exists . . . shall find its perfection and fulfillment in him" (Eph. 1:10, Phillips). We shall reach "the measure of the stature of the fulness of Christ" (Eph. 4:13, KJV).

AFTERWORD

We may not say now that we have the answers. Questions of how to conduct oneself as a Christian, or how to serve as a Christian, must be answered by life itself— the life of the individual in his direct, responsible relationship to God. This is a dynamic, never a static, thing. And how can we speak at all of the true meaning of conduct and service if we do not speak first and last of love? For it is love which sums up all other commands. The one who loves knows better than anyone else how to conduct himself, how to serve the one he loves. Love prescribes an answer in a given situation as no mere rule can do.

"The man whose life is lived in love does, in fact, live in God, and God does, in fact, live in him."

For Further Reading

BETWEEN A ROCK AND A HARD PLACE. By Mark O. Hatfield. The personal manifesto of the senior senator from Oregon, declaring the focus of his faith in Christ. In soul-searching honesty, he wrestles with today's crucial issues: violence, "just war," civil religion, the centralization of power, preserving the environment, poverty and hunger. Old and New Testaments are combed to provide a biblical understanding of church-state relations. #80427.

CONFLICT AND CONSCIENCE. By Mark O. Hatfield. Senator Hatfield talks about some of his most deeply held beliefs, both his political convictions (which he calls "the consequence rather than the cause of my life's basic orientation") and his personal faith. #80227 (hardback); #90026 (paperback).